Treasured Echoes

Divya Shiji

BookLeaf Publishing
India | USA | UK

Presentation by *BookLeaf Publishing*

Web: www.bookleafpub.com

E-mail: info@bookleafpub.com

ISBN: 9789363318403

First edition 2024

Dedication

To my dearest family, whose boundless love and unwavering support have been the light and heartbeat guiding me through every word and verse.

ACKNOWLEDGEMENT

I would like to extend my heartfelt gratitude to all those who have supported me throughout the creation of this book, *"Treasured Echoes."*

First and foremost, I want to express my deepest appreciation to my Lord Almighty for guiding me every step of the way. I am immensely grateful to my parents, Papa and Mumma, for their unwavering love, encouragement, and understanding. Their support has been my rock throughout this journey.

To my beloved family—my Achachan Shiji Thomas and my children, Ashale and Oshana—thank you for being my constant source of inspiration and strength. Your presence fills each day with joy and purpose. A very special thanks to my husband, Shiji Thomas, for always standing by me and supporting every step I take. My children, in particular, have been a tremendous source of support and inspiration, encouraging and believing in me every step of the way.

Special thanks to my in-laws, Papa and Mumma; my loving brother Dipin K. A., his wonderful wife and steadfast supporter Linta, and their delightful children, Johaan and Joshua. I am also deeply grateful to my beautiful sister-in-law Shiny Varghese, her husband and my mentor Saju Varghese, and their beloved kids Steffi and Neil, who have all been a great support.

My sincere thanks extend to all my family relatives, friends, and mentors who have supported me in my poetic journey. Though there are too many names to list individually, please know that your encouragement and belief in me have meant the world.

To all the readers who embark on this poetic voyage with me, thank you for your time and for allowing my words to touch your hearts. Your support means everything to me.

Lastly, I want to express my gratitude to everyone who, knowingly and unknowingly, has helped bring my vision to life and given me the courage and strength to pursue my passion despite the challenges.

This book is a testament to the power of community, love, and the written word. Thank you, from the bottom of my heart, for being a part of this incredible journey.

Heartfelt regards,

Divya

PREFACE

Welcome to "Treasured Echoes," a collection of poems that have journeyed from the quiet corners of my heart to the pages of this book. Each poem in this anthology holds a piece of my soul, crafted from moments of introspection and inspired by the profound experiences of life.

Many of these poems found their beginnings on my website, My Space: A Journey Towards Self-Discovery, where I first ventured into the art of expressing my innermost thoughts. Now, with gratitude and humility, I present them to you in the form of my second poetry book, "Treasured Echoes."

A Reflection of Life's Journey

Within these pages, you will find reflections on love, resilience, and the beauty of embracing one's true self. Each poem serves as a mirror, inviting you to explore the labyrinth of emotions that define our human experience. From gentle whispers of self-discovery to resounding echoes of inner strength, this collection celebrates the complexity and richness of life.

Accompanied by Wisdom

Accompanying these verses are carefully curated quotes, like guiding stars in the night sky. They illuminate the path to understanding and enlightenment, offering insights that complement the emotional depth of each poem. Together, these words and reflections aim to evoke contemplation and inspire a deeper connection with oneself and the world around us.

Journey Shared

As you embark on this poetic journey, may these words resonate within you, stirring the echoes of your own thoughts and emotions. May they serve as companions on your own path of self-discovery, offering solace, strength, and a renewed appreciation for the beauty of introspection.

Thank you for joining me in this exploration of "Treasured Echoes." May these poems find a place in your heart as they have in mine.

A Childhood Without Toys

In childhood's tender hours, I longed for toys so dear,
Dreams filled with colorful joy, but reality was clear,
No treasures in my hands, no playthings to enjoy,
Yet I found happiness in simple things. Oh, what a joy!

Paper, stones, cardboard boxes, my precious toys,
Imagination sprouts out in many humble joys
I cherished every moment, in every simple thing,
Creating a world of wonder just like anything.

I prayed for just one toy, one cherished little friend,
But fate had different plans, a message it did send,
My childhood, forged in simple ways, with heart and soul I'd play,
And even in the absence of toys, I found my special way.

But now, as a parent, I watch my daughter with a smile,
She is surrounded by toys, mile by mile.
She hardly cares for one, always wanting for more,
While I yearned for just one, as in dreams of yore,

Oh, how long can I play with those toys?
To relish the joys they give that I never enjoy.
Forgetting time, forgetting age,
Lost in a world where fantasies engage.

Through my daughter's eyes, I now perceive,
For in wanting and in having, we chase a common dream,
Yet in my humble journey, I've come to understand,
That in the absence of it all, I held life in my hand.

Getting nothing, getting everything, sailing on the same tide,
In the search for something more, we journey far and wide,
But beauty lies in moments, in love, and in grace,
Even without toys, we find our special place.

P.S. This poem was written as a reflection on my own childhood experiences and the realization that happiness can be found in simplicity and imagination, even in the absence of material possessions like toys. It serves as a reminder to cherish the moments and treasures of life beyond the pursuit of material wealth and to find joy in the little things that often go unnoticed.

Quote: "In the absence of everything I desired, I held life in my hand."

Imperfections' Shine

Imperfection, a word we all dislike,
Yet within us, it secretly lies,
An act we commit, no one can deny,
But why does imperfection make one cry?

Perfection, the ideal, is what we strive to be.
But in our journey, we often can't see.
That beauty lies in our flaws, don't you see?
Embrace your imperfections and set yourself
free.

Wabi-sabi, a lesson to find light,
In its imperfection, it's a delight
Happiness lies not in creating perfect themes
But accept each of our flawed themes.

So let us embrace our imperfect souls.
As life's masterpiece unfolds,
For imperfection when held with grace,
It becomes the art that lights up our space.

The wabi-sabi concept is a Japanese philosophy that celebrates imperfect beauty. Nothing lasts, nothing is finished, and nothing is perfect.

P.S. This poem was born out of a reflection on the human struggle with imperfection and the profound beauty found within it. It's a reminder that, in a world obsessed with flawlessness, our imperfections are what make us unique and endearing. Embracing imperfection is not just about self-acceptance; it's about recognizing the inherent beauty in life's asymmetry and unpredictability. May this poem serve as a gentle nudge to embracc our imperfect selves and find solace in the wabi-sabi of existence.

Quote: "Embrace the cracks and flaws, for they tell the story of a tired soul. In the imperfection, we discover a unique kind of beauty that resonates with the rhythm of life itself."

Memories that Tickle My Nose

In a world of scents, where memories lay,
My olfactory senses lead the way.
With every fragrance that tickles my nose,
A rush of stories, close in tow it goes.

Each scent unravels tales of the old days,
Untying the knots of life's mysterious ways.
A summer rain, on a scorching day's heat,
It takes me back to childhood, with friends so sweet.

The aroma of coffee, warm and inviting,
It turns lazy mornings into enlightening stories.
And the aroma of curries, so refined,
Brings forth mom's taste, memories unwind.

Fresh grass after rainfall, a scent so pure,
It takes me to the park, where joy would endure.
Frankincense smoke, floating high in the sky,
Unveils family gatherings, where spirits would fly.

The fragrance of books, wise and aged,
Leads me to libraries, where knowledge is engaged.
And the scent of ink, so subtle and crisp,
Revives the hostel days, a treasure I miss.

My sense of smell, a powerful guide,
Unlocks doors to moments where time can't hide.
For as fragrances find me, vibrant and strong,
I'm swept to where I belong—where I truly belong.

P.S. This poem was written to celebrate the often-overlooked power of our sense of smell to trigger memories and emotions. It's a reminder that, amidst the chaos of life, there's a world of wonder waiting to be explored through the scents that surround us. Each fragrance carries with it a story, a memory, a piece of our past that shapes who we are. So let's embrace the beauty of scent and allow it to transport us to the places where we truly belong.

Quote: "Sometimes, my sense of smell sweeps me away to the place where my heart truly belongs."

The Thoughtless Girl

There once was a thoughtless girl, you see.
Her mind was empty, void of empathy.
No thoughts danced, and no ideas came.
She blocked every thought, like a scary dream.

Some called her careless, a mindless being,
But she was merely thoughtless, with thoughts flying.
Is it good or bad, this vacant mind state?
The emptiness and lightness it creates.

Yet in her emptiness, a light seems to shine.
simple, pure, extremely divine,
In this absence, nothing unfolds.
Still, flowers bloom in her empty world.

So judge her not; this thoughtlessness is so clear,
She has found happiness in the vacant air.
A lesson she teaches, though strange it may
seem,
Sometimes it's okay to let go of the dream.

P.S. This poem was written as a gentle reminder to embrace the complexities of human existence, including moments of emptiness or thoughtlessness. It seeks to challenge the common perception that a busy mind is always a productive or fulfilling one. Instead, it suggests that sometimes, in letting go of the incessant chatter of our thoughts, we can find peace, simplicity, and even happiness. It encourages us to appreciate beauty in moments of quiet clarity, where simplicity and lightness reign supreme.

Quote: "The beauty of an empty mind is so pure, that sometimes it is good to let go of the dreams."

Unseen Gestures

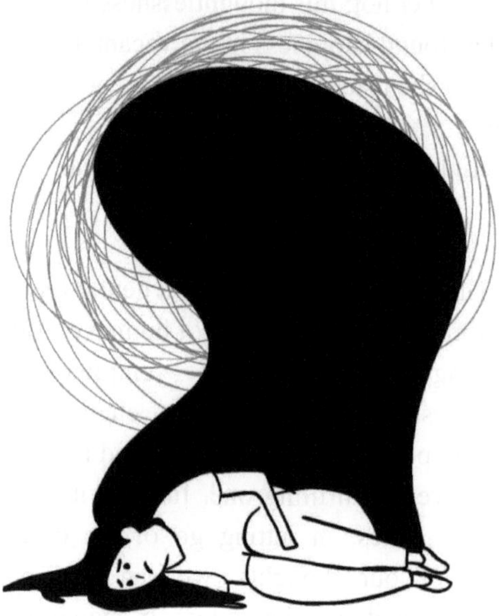

I tried everything to catch your eye,
But you ignored my every try.
Now that I've stopped doing it for you,
You finally noticed that I did nothing for you.

I waited for your appreciation to come.
But your compliments never came.
And now, for everything I do,
You express disappointment, my heart is aching so.

I longed for your smile, a simple gesture,
But you are never bothered or ignored
Now that I don't see your way,
You complain, feeling I no longer stay.

It's the simple act of being there,
That shows you truly love and care.
For husband and wife, sibling and friend,
May we all aim to interrupt this trend.

Let us strive to give time, to show that we care,
So that when we're in need, someone will be
there.
A little effort can bridge these divides.
Creating a bond that nothing can break.

P.S. This poem was written as a reminder of the importance of recognizing and appreciating the unseen gestures of love and care in our relationships. Often, it's the small acts of kindness, the quiet support, and the moments of presence that truly strengthen our connections with others. In a busy world where attention is easily diverted, it's crucial to pause and acknowledge the efforts made by our loved ones, lest we inadvertently take them for granted. May this poem inspire us all to cherish and reciprocate the unnoticed expressions of affection that enrich our lives.

Quote: "Give your time generously in nurturing relationships, for what you give is what you get."

How I Love My Space in Sleep

In the land of dreams, I find my way,
A space where I love to enjoy and play,
I'm the hero—bold and free,
In adventures that are just for me.

When daylight breaks, I still hold tight
My dreams shine so bright,
Throughout the day, they light my way,
Chasing worries, keeping them away.

In a little boy's world, a place to enjoy,
In that special place, my dreams are full of joy,
I cherish each moment, where I'm the king,
Oh, how I love my space in sleep; it's
everything!

In my dreams, I'm always the star.
Chasing adventures, no matter how far,
A small boy's joy, like a flowing stream,
In that special place where I live my dream.

P.S. This poem was written as a celebration of the magical realm of dreams, where we can escape the confines of reality and embrace our innermost desires and aspirations. It's a reminder of the importance of holding onto our dreams, even when faced with the challenges of everyday life. Dreams have the power to inspire us, uplift our spirits, and fuel our creativity, serving as a sanctuary where we can be whoever we want to be. So, let us cherish and embrace the enchanting world of dreams, for it is a space where our imaginations can truly soar.

Quote: "Dreams are the gateway to the world of imagination, where every soul can be a hero."

Empathy

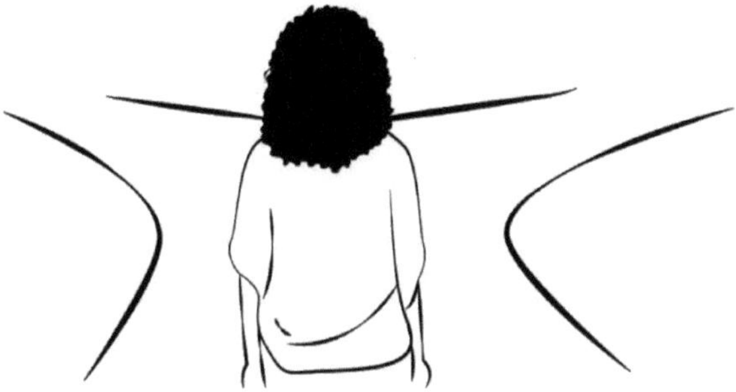

In the journey of motherhood, I fall short,
I was unable to guess their every thought.
But that's okay; I'm not a mind reader, you see,
I'll be their faithful friend and let them be free.

For I long to be their friend, always true,
Where they can pour their hearts out without a clue,
Knowing they're heard, without a single regret,
Unafraid to share feelings, a bond they won't forget.

But sometimes, my children struggle too.
To grasp the depths of all that I do.
Yet that's alright; they're not mind readers as well.
But they can try to understand and hear me as well.

For in seeking to understand, you'll learn to
perceive,
The depth of emotions that others may weave.
A listener, a friend, you'll become day by day,
A skill that will guide you along life's way.

To be there for others, through highs and lows,
With a gentle understanding that truly shows,
Sometimes words fail, but hearts can mend,
And being a good listener is a gift that won't
end.

Let us journey together, dear,
This bond will grow and deepen, crystal clear.
For understanding and empathy, they will see,
Are the pillars that will nurture them, and me,
you see.

P.S. This poem was written as a gentle reminder that in the journey of motherhood, as well as in any relationship, empathy is a vital ingredient. It's a recognition that we may not always understand each other perfectly, but by striving to listen, empathize, and support one another, we can forge stronger bonds and navigate life's ups and downs with compassion and understanding.

Quote: "Motherhood isn't about having all the answers; it's about a shared journey of discovery with her kids."

Who Stole My Time?

Who stole my time, I ask, in despair,
Always prepared, yet unable to bear
The weight of my tasks, lingering in line,
Someone has taken my precious time.

Before the clock strikes, I'm set to go.
But still, I arrive with minutes to show.
Cold food on my plate, no warmth to delight,
For time has been stolen, stolen from sight.

My daily routine, a hurried affair.
No time to spare, no moments to share,
With parents dear, longing for a chime,
But stolen is time; it's no longer mine.

I'm damn busy, with no seconds to spare.
Burdened by duties beyond what's fair,
This thief unseen, who holds a great crime,
I must find the culprit who stole my time.

Oh! look and see, it's my mobile device,
A shameless thief, with its tempting voice,
Scrolling and swiping, stealing away,
Each passing moment, day after day.

Oh, mobile, how could you be so bold?
To steal my time, as the hours unfold,
Our relationship untied; it's time to break free.
To save my time and reclaim what should be.

So farewell, dear phone, with all its allure.
I'll reclaim my moments, my time that's pure,
No longer enslaved, I'll let my life rhyme.
For no one will steal again, my precious time.

P.S. This poem was born from a realization that our most precious commodity, time, can easily slip away unnoticed. In the modern age, with endless distractions vying for our attention, it's all too easy to lose sight of what truly matters. Through this poem, I hope to shed light on the insidious thief that often robs us of our time: our mobile devices and the addictive allure of technology. It serves as a reminder to prioritize our moments, reclaim control over our schedules, and cherish the precious time we have with loved ones and in pursuing our passions.

Quote: "Time is a thief that snatches moments when we are not looking."

Oh, the Lazy Day!!

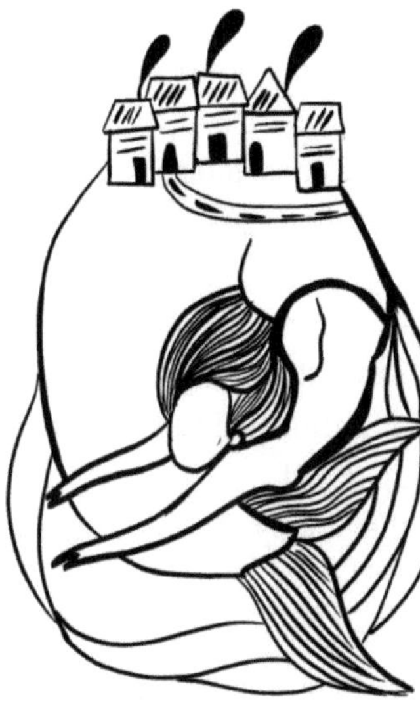

On a long, lazy day, time doesn't seem to end,
As we struggle to wait for the day to reach its end.
No motivation to rise from our cozy bed,
Just content to lie there with no thoughts in our heads.

No hunger to eat, no thirst for a drink,
Just lost in comfort, not wanting to think.
A day of pure leisure, a rare chance to live
But deep down, we know that laziness.

Tomorrow may come with its tasks and its chores,
The burden of laziness will visit us no more.
Yet in these moments of idleness, we find solace,
Not realizing the consequences until tomorrow's face.

It's easy to waste a day in leisure's way,
But the following day brings a piling display.
The weight of unfinished tasks, an overwhelming dread,
A reminder that a long, lazy day leaves much to be said.

So let us cherish these moments, few and far between,
But remember the balance that must be seen.
A touch of relaxation, a sprinkle of ease,
But with a touch of productivity, to put our minds at ease.

So indulge in today's laziness, let it take hold,
But as the sun sets, let tomorrow unfold.
Strike a balance between rest and toil.
A life of harmony is what we all truly long for.

P.S. This poem was born out of a reflection on the delicate dance between leisure and productivity in our lives. It serves as a gentle reminder to appreciate those rare moments of laziness while also acknowledging the importance of maintaining a balance between relaxation and responsibility. By capturing the essence of a lazy day, it encourages readers to embrace moments of rest while being mindful of the consequences of excessive idleness. Ultimately, it aims to inspire a deeper appreciation for both leisure and productivity, guiding us towards a more harmonious way of living.

Quote: "Balance the art of life, where lazy days and productive moments together create a masterpiece of fulfillment."

Buying Worry, Earning Wrinkles

As we grow older, signs start to appear.
Reminders of time, and the passing of years,
Our bodies, once vibrant, now show wear and tear,
And these signs of aging concern me, dear.

We strive to hide them or seek remedies new.
To overcome wrinkles and keep youth in view,
But sometimes these signs stubbornly get in you,
For aging is a part of life, it's true.

But let us wonder: why do we grow in age?
Were the kids, so effortlessly, turning a new
page,
With bodies untouched by time's cruel wage,
They hop and they laugh, embracing life's stage.

The reason, my friends, lies within our quest.
For worries and troubles, they burden our chests,
We forget to enjoy, to live our very best,
And instead, we sit idly, with worries as our
guest.

So let's be like kids, carefree and kind.
Bid farewell to worries that cloud our mind,
Hop around, laugh, and all emotions to find.
Embrace life's beauty, leave no joy behind.

And as we age gracefully, with each passing day,
Let beauty shine through, in our own special
way,
Signs of aging hold beauty, some say,
A testament to wisdom, come that way.

So let us not fear these signs that appear,
For within them lie stories, memories so dear,
And as we age gracefully, our spirits shall cheer,
Embracing life's journey without any fear.

P.S. This poem, "Buying Worry, Earning Wrinkles," was born from a reflection on the human experience of aging and the societal pressures surrounding it. It's a reminder to myself and others that while aging may bring physical changes, it's our mindset and approach to life that truly define us. I wrote this to encourage embracing the beauty of aging, to celebrate the wisdom it brings, and to remind us all to live each moment fully without letting worries steal our joy.

Quote: "Aging is a process of painting where a canvas is adorned with different kinds of memories and experiences, each wrinkle and line adding the beautiful finishing touches to the masterpiece of life well lived."

How My Mind Wanders

Many times I forget as things slip through my
mind.
The most urgent tasks, often left behind.
They label me careless, a fool without a care,
But truth be told, sometimes my mind's not
there.

Like broken glass, my thoughts scatter wide.
When my brain takes a break, they collide.
They label me lazy, lacking grace,
Yet it's the chaos within me I face.

It's not my fault, this playful brain's game,
Avoiding pathways, it's not the same.
In this race against time, I'm not alone,
In forgetfulness, we've all grown.

So don't judge my forgetfulness, my absentminded phase,
Beneath this scattered surface, a thinker holds its place.
Seeking peace in chaos, finding to get out of this cause,
Hoping to tame thoughts in life's ever-changing chase.

P.S. This poem, "How My Mind Wanders," was written as a reflection on the experience of forgetfulness and absent-mindedness. It's a reminder that while some may perceive these traits as signs of carelessness or laziness, they often stem from the inherent complexities of the mind and the constant juggling of tasks and thoughts. By sharing these words, the aim is to foster understanding and empathy towards those who navigate the chaos within their minds, seeking peace amidst the storm.

Quotes: "Where the mind often stumbles in regret, we may sometimes seek excuses."

The Endless Obsession

In a world of screens, my story begins,
When I got a new phone, my obsession had no end.
Lost in its pixels, I couldn't hear or see,
Caught in a whirlpool of virtual fantasy.

My parents, worried, would scold and advise,
"Don't be consumed; look around and open your eyes!
The world around you is a wonder to explore.
Don't let it pass; there's so much more."

But I brushed them off, my confidence near.
“No need to look elsewhere; my phone is here.
The world resides within it; my window so wide,
Through its virtual land, I peacefully slide."

Yet time moved swiftly, as it always will.
And tables turned, a cycle to fill.
Now I see my parents, caught in digital art,
Phones in hand, a world held close to the heart.

I told them now, with concern in my voice,
“Look up from your screens, make a different choice.
The world is out there, full of beauty untold,
Embrace it now, before it gets too old.”

They respond with a smile, a knowing glance,
“Dear child, don't worry; give life a chance.
The world resides within this little device.
Through its lens, we see wonders arise."

And so the cycle spins in an endless way.
As we share our lives, day after day.
Phones in hand, lost in rare zones,
Forgetting that life is more than just phones.

Let us break this digital trance,
And find balance, give reality a chance.
Embrace the world, both near and far,
True connections will always be the brightest star.

P.S. This poem was written as a gentle reminder to myself and others about the importance of finding balance in our relationship with technology. It's easy to get lost in the digital world and overlook the beauty and richness of the world around us. Through this poem, I hope to encourage reflection on our digital habits and inspire a greater appreciation for the wonders of real-life experiences and connections.

Quote: "Lost on the Screen: A Tale of Endless Obsession"

Sometimes it's okay

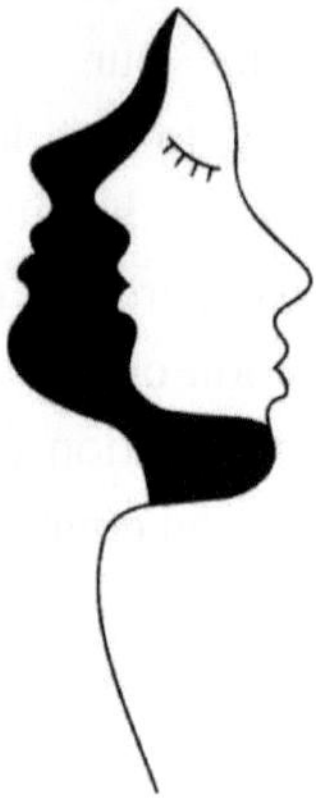

Sometimes it's okay; we all understand.
Just to let go of the rules, just for the brand.
Be honest and truthful; that's what we know.
But sometimes it's okay to let feelings show.

Respect others always; that's the way.
But sometimes it's okay to have a bad day.
Be kind, be responsible—these are the values we hold.
But sometimes it's okay to break the mold.

Understanding is key; to walk in their shoes,
But sometimes it's okay to take a break, to choose.
Justice, the pillar upon which we stand,
But sometimes it's harder to take a firm stand.

Help others, lend a hand when they're weak,
But sometimes it's okay to be the one who seeks.
Lies and stealing should never be in a play.
But sometimes it's okay to let go of the gray.

Never harm others; that's the golden rule.
But sometimes it's okay to join self-defense school.
Love everyone, regardless of shades or who we see.
But sometimes it's okay to let go and just be free.

So let go of the pressure and expectations so high.
Because sometimes it's okay to kiss the sky.
Live your life authentically, be true to your soul,
For sometimes it's okay to let go and lose control.

Let's embrace the beauty of imperfection.
For sometimes it's okay to deviate from our direction.
So remember, my friend, to embrace both light and dark.
For sometimes it's okay to create your own spark.

P.S. This poem was written as a gentle reminder that while it's essential to uphold values, principles, and responsibilities, it's also crucial to acknowledge our humanity. Life isn't always black and white; there are moments when we need to allow ourselves the grace to deviate from the usual path, to acknowledge our vulnerabilities, and to embrace our authenticity. It's a reminder that it's okay not to always have it all together and that finding a balance between structure and spontaneity is part of the beautiful journey of being human.

Quote: "Sometimes it's okay to choose certain shades of flexibility to craft the art of a meaningful journey."

The Shades of Green

In the garden of life, I stood and sighed.
The age-old tale, "The Grass is Greener on the other side,"
A whispering delusion; it echoed so loud,
Yet within my heart, a different truth vowed

The grass appeared lush, verdant, and bold.
Beyond compare in the neighbor's plot.
But on closer inspection, I began to see
My own patch of green caught my eye.

Underneath the sun's gentle rays,
My grass, too, wore emerald rays.
Each blade whispered tales of its might.
Yet my eyes yearned for a different sight.

I questioned the whispers that clouded my view,
Why yearn for others' green when mine is true?
Comparisons and envy clouded my soul.
Yet the essence of my being held a unique role.

The sunsets painted a canvas so divine,
On my side of the fence, they began to shine.
The laughter that echoed in the air I breathed,
In my own patch of green, it shined like
anything.

No, the grass wasn't barren or dull, I found.
It was the lens I wore, a disguise I was bound,
Shifting my focus, altering my lens,
Revealed the beauty that was mine now and
then.

I chose to water my grass, nurture it well,
In my story, in my truth, I began to dwell,
And as the days unfolded, my vision improved.
I embraced my shade of green—a life I loved.

So let the world believe in the mirage they see.
The grass is greener; it's an illusion. Let it be.
On the canvas of life, my colors blend and
blend.
And in my own shades of green, my soul likes to
mend.

P.S. This poem, "The Shades of Green," was penned as a reminder to myself and others that the perception of greener grass elsewhere often stems from a distorted lens through which we view our own lives. It's a reflection on the tendency to compare and envy, and the realization that true contentment lies in nurturing and appreciating the beauty within our own existence. May it serve as a gentle nudge to embrace our unique journey and find solace in the vibrant hues of our own patch of green.

Quote: "The belief that 'grass is greener on the other side' was my delusion yet alone, as my own grass was green as well. It's not about what I had, but how I felt within."

Half Empty or Half Full

In a moment of reflection,
With a glass of water, a simple connection,
I sipped half of it, feeling content.
But my thoughts took a different bent.

The glass in my hand, its contents shrink,
An age-old debate ignites: what do I think?
Is it half empty, a sign of lacking,
Or half full, a story worth everything?

A choice to be made in each passing day,
To perceive life's essence in a balanced way.
For the glass, the water, the liquid so pure,
Teaches us lessons and wisdom to endure.

A whisper inside me, a gentle voice,
Reminded me of the power of choice,
A half-empty mindset breeds despair.
While half-full thinking lifts us beyond compare.

Life's winding road, its peaks, and its falls
Can either break or sculpt our inner walls,
With half-empty vision, joy seems far,
Yet half-full hearts dream under the star.

So, I chose the path that spreads its light.
To paint my life with colors so bright,
With gratitude and strength as my guide,
I embraced the journey, the highs, and the tide.

For it's not the glass but how we perceive,
The wonders of each moment we receive
Whether half-empty or half-full, it's our view,
Our outlook shapes life, old and new.

So, let us choose, with courage and might,
Grasping hope in the darkest night,
In this very choice, our true power was found.
Rise above with each step from the ground.

P.S. This poem, "Half Empty or Half Full," was written as a gentle reminder to myself and to anyone who reads it that our perspective shapes our reality. It was born from a moment of reflection where I realized the profound impact our outlook can have on our experiences and how we navigate through life's challenges. By choosing to see the glass as half full, we embrace optimism, resilience, and gratitude, which can guide us through even the darkest of times. May this poem serve as a beacon of light, encouraging us all to choose positivity and hope in every moment we encounter.

Quote: "Half Empty or Half Full" is the choice of perception between half empty and half full one can have in the same situation."

A Taste of Everything

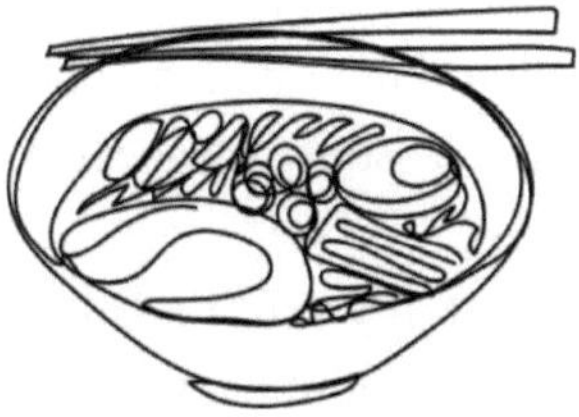

Lord plated everything I needed on my plate,
Along with all I don't need, that's fate.
At first, I'd select what I'd want and what not.
But as I grew up, I realized my thoughts.

Whatever is being served, I need to have.
To learn and evolve, my soul must carve
For within each bite lies a lesson true.
A chance to grow and embrace the new

A feast of experiences, flavors divine,
Nourishing my spirit, one meal at a time
I embrace the abundance that life designed.
No longer confined by a restrictive mind.

On this divine platter, blessings unfold.
From savory to sweet, stories untold
Every bite is a journey, a new adventure,
A taste of life's essence, a delight to quench
more

Lord plated abundance, both bitter and sweet,
For in every challenge, growth we meet.
So I savor each moment with an open heart.
Appreciating the lessons, a true work of art.

In this grand feast, my soul finds its way.
Through trials and triumphs, I have learned
many ways.
With gratitude, I took part in life's play.
Lord's platter, a gift, guiding my pathway.

Thank you for the feast; the flavors are so vast.
In this grand feast, I'm steadfast.
Grateful for the variety; it looks so bright.
Lord, I cherish every moment, day and night.

P.S. This poem, "A Taste of Everything," was written as a reflection on the journey of life and the realization that every experience, whether joyful or challenging, contributes to our growth and evolution. It serves as a reminder to embrace the abundance of life with gratitude and an open heart, recognizing that each moment, like a bite from a diverse platter, offers us the opportunity to learn, evolve, and appreciate the richness of existence.

Quote: "Life is a grand feast, and we must taste everything it offers to appreciate its rich flavor."

Every Day is a Day

Every day brings new possibilities, so bright,
Yet we struggle to finish the ones from before.
Everyday is a fresh start, a new light,
Yet old chapters keep us bound and unsure.

Every day brings hope, a ray of gold,
But still, we battle with our hopelessness.
Everyday shines, stories yet untold,
Yet darkness stays, leaving us in distress.

End it all before you go to sleep.
And wake up to a new version each day.
Smile, hope, and new dreams in leap
Embrace life's offerings, come what may.

Everyday is a gift, unspoiled and pure.
With each sunrise comes a chance to start anew.
So seize the moment and let your spirit soar.
And bask in the wonders life offers you.

P.S. This poem was written as a reminder that while each day presents us with new opportunities and fresh beginnings, it's also important to acknowledge and address the challenges and burdens carried over from the past. It's a call to embrace the beauty of each day while recognizing the struggles that may persist, urging readers to find strength and hope in the face of adversity.

Quote: "Every day is a day to make a choice, to live with a purpose, and to embrace the opportunities it brings."

The Art of Saying No

No to the hate that divides us apart,
No to the judgment that breaks the heart.
No to the anger that fuels the fire,
No to the violence that brings the dire.

For when we say no, we create a space,
For love and compassion to take their place.
We open our hearts and lend a hand,
We heal the wounds and rebuild the land.

No is the voice that speaks for peace,
No is the hope that helps us release.
No is the dream that we hold dear,
No is the vision that brings us near.

So let us foster the art of saying no,
And see how far its strength can go.
For in its might, we find our light,
No holding us back from shining bright.

No to the darkness that clouds the mind,
No to the ignorance that leaves us blind.
No to the despair that sinks our soul,
No to the hate that takes its toll.

For when we say no, we stand for love,
Unconditional, pure, and from above.
We unite as one and lift each other,
Together we rise and emerge stronger.

So let us foster the art of saying no,
And let it guide us as we grow.
For in its strength, we find our way,
To a brighter future, come what may.

P.S. This poem was born from a deep reflection on the power of saying no in a world often dominated by negativity and division. It was crafted as a reminder that saying no isn't just about rejection; it's about making space for what truly matters—love, compassion, and unity. In a time when hate, judgment, and anger seem prevalent, this poem serves as a beacon of hope, urging us to stand firm in our values and embrace the transformative potential of saying no to what diminishes us and yes to what uplifts us.

Quote: "Learn the art of saying 'no' to pave your path to 'yes' where it counts the most."

Unnoticed Tears

"Oh, tears unannounced, arriving untold,
Without a whisper, you start to unfold.
In sadness, you come, yet in happiness too.
A paradox within, both old and new

You are with me every time, unseen and true.
If someone is in pain, you emerge to see their
view.
If someone is joyful, you reveal their happiness.
On every occasion, you come without a trace.

If someone is triumphant, you reveal yourself.
If someone is defeated, you emerge as well.
For all my emotions, you stand by my side.
Yet touched by others' pain with your tide.

I can't understand you many times; it's true.
Your purpose is elusive, like a hidden clue.
Yet through the thunderous tide of life's rain,
You flow seamlessly, touching hearts again and again.

Love and emotions together, arranged
Joy and sorrow delicately get engaged.
Hope springs eternally as your presence stays,
Invisible threads bind caring souls' ways.

Though labeled "unnoticed," your power prevails.
Transcending borders of joy and despair
Whispering comfort to whose weep unheard,
Igniting hope for all who dare to bear

The weight of emotion that life owns
In several moments, it travels too long.
Oh, tears unnoticed yet felt deeply so true,
Your essence sings a bittersweet song we all knew.

P.S. This poem, "Unnoticed Tears," was born from a desire to explore the profound yet often overlooked role that tears play in our lives. It was written to remind us of the intricate tapestry of emotions that shape our existence and to honor the silent strength of tears in expressing the depths of joy, sorrow, triumph, and defeat. Through its verses, I sought to capture the essence of tears as both a universal language of the heart and a powerful force that binds us together in our shared humanity.

Quote: "Tears, a constant unnoticed companion of our journey."

REBOOT

In the chaos of our daily lives,
When we're trapped in a web of thoughts,
Bogged down by the weight of negativity,
Oh, how I wish we had a reboot button.

Like a computer system, we could reset,
Clearing out the unwanted clutter,
Reloading ourselves to a pristine state,
Ready to function at our very best.

Just imagine the power to let go.
Of all the hurtful words and doubts,
To silence the critics that haunt our minds,
With a simple click, a reset, a reboot

But alas, such a button is not within us.
We cannot escape our own tangled thoughts.
Yet still, there's a way to find solace.
To reboot ourselves amidst the storm.

Close your eyes, oh my dear friend.
Breathe deep and declutter your mind.
Focus on self-care with mindfulness,
Let meditation be your guide.

Each of us has our own unique way.
To find that internal reboot button,
To shed the weight of the world,
And emerge stronger, rejuvenated.

Let's look for that reset within.
Life's challenges weigh us down.
Reboot ourselves with love and kindness,
And watch as our spirits soar and abound.

In this journey of self-renewal,
Let's find the audacity to let go.
To embrace the power of rebooting,
And become the best versions of ourselves we know.

P.S. This poem, "REBOOT" was written as a reminder that amidst the chaos and challenges of life, we often yearn for a reset button to escape negativity and doubt. It serves as a gentle nudge to recognize that while we may not have a literal reboot button, we possess the capacity to rejuvenate ourselves internally. The poem encourages embracing practices like mindfulness and self-care to declutter our minds and emerge stronger. It was penned with the hope of inspiring others to find their own ways of resetting and becoming the best versions of themselves.

Quote: "Within the chaos, we yearn for a reboot—a chance to shed the old, cleanse our spirit, and embrace the promise of new beginnings."

Dream Again

I can't accept myself as this.
I have dreamt of something different for myself.
I am suffocating, looking up like this.
I want my dreams back. Oh, how I wish!

But years have passed, and I became this.
How can I be my dream when I am old?
I can't turn back time; I can't rewind the clock.
Still, a ray of hope in me holds.

It asks me to step out of me.
To try and draw my dream as I want it to be.
Yes, I know it's not that easy.
It's the toughest thing I'll ever see.

But trust me, as I finish my drawing,
And I look at it with my eyes wide open.
I would be jolly and thrilled to see
The transformation that changed me was
unspoken.

For it is in the act of creation,
I find solace and liberation.
In the strokes of my pen, the colors of my soul,
I can become the person I've always longed to
know.

So let me pick up that pen and that brush.
And paint my dreams without a hush.
On this canvas of life, I'll find my way.
And let my true self come to play.

Though the journey may be tough,
The path may seem unclear,
I will keep pushing forward.
With determination and no fear.

In the act of drawing my dreams,
I'll uncover strength I never knew.
And with each stroke, each line, and each shade,
A transformation will ensue.

So, dreamer, fear not the passing years.

It's never too late to chase what's dear.
Trust in yourself, embrace the unknown,
And watch as your dreams slowly appear.

In the end, as I step back and see,
The masterpiece that is now me
I'll be overwhelmed with joy and pride.
As I dream again and become what I've always tried to be.

P.S. This poem was written as a reminder to myself and to all those who may feel trapped by the passage of time or the weight of their past choices. It serves as a gentle nudge to embrace the power of creation, to pick up the tools of our imagination, and to paint our dreams anew on the canvas of life. It's a testament to the resilience of the human spirit and the infinite capacity we possess to reinvent ourselves, regardless of our age or circumstances. So, to anyone feeling disheartened or stuck, remember that within the act of dreaming again lies the potential for profound transformation and fulfillment.

Quote: "Dream again, for within your dreams, you will find the key to a brighter reality."

Happily Ever After

Today, I will reveal my childhood belief,
A treasure cherished within, a lifelong relief.
I believe in fairy tales, my heart holds dear.
Where dreams come alive, hope is always near.

I believe in the magic they weave.
In enchanted forests where dreams conceive,
Where heroes rise and villains deceive,
And love's pure light, the darkness reprieve.

For in every tale, a single refrain
Echo softly, like a summer rain,
"They lived happily ever after," it proclaims.
It's a beacon of hope amidst life's strain.

Through turbulent storms and despair's abyss,
I cling to this belief, a steadfast wish,
No matter what trials I must face,
A moment will come, a saving grace.

Every trial must come to an end.
A new chapter of the story will be sent.
To a place where joy knows no amend,
Where happiness reigns, my heart will mend.

So I journey on, with this belief in tow.
Through valleys of sorrow and mountains of woe,
Deep within this knowledge, I know,
That my own "happily ever after" will grow.

And though the path may twist and bend,
I know that love will guide me, my friend.
For in the tales of old, the message is clear:
That hope is eternal, conquering fear.

So, I march forward with a hopeful heart.
Knowing that my fairy tale, too, will start,
A new chapter, where joy will impart,
And I'll live happily ever after, with all my heart.

P.S. I wrote this poem, "Happily Ever After," to celebrate and reaffirm my childhood belief in fairy tales. It reflects my enduring faith in the power of hope and love to conquer adversity. Through the verses, I wanted to convey the message that, despite life's challenges, there is always a possibility for happiness and renewal. May this poem inspire others to hold onto their dreams and believe in their own "happily ever after."

Quote: "Embrace the magic of fairy tales, where hope blooms eternally and dreams find their happily ever after."

The Bamboo on My Fence

My beautiful garden, so lush and green,
Bamboo on my fence—a serene scene.
Nature's wisdom, a silent sentinel's grace,
In its quiet strength, a valuable embrace

Single stems rising, tall and strong,
Neighbors grow freely, to nature's song.
In life's hurry-burry a symphony to play,
Bamboo dances through night and day.

With each breeze, it gracefully sways.
In storms and rain, it humbly obeys.
Bending, twisting, allowing the flow,
Yet, at its core, it has an unwavering glow.

Lessons whispered in the bamboo's sigh,
Adapt to life's twists as time passes by.
Sway with the tides; let your spirit soar.
Stand tall, stay strong at your very core.

Resilience lives in the bamboo's embrace.
A reminder of life's ever-changing grace.
In the face of trials, we find our song.
With flexibility, we all belong.

So, let the bamboo on my fence inspire.
With its quiet strength, we can acquire
The wisdom to bend and gracefully endure,
With unwavering strength, we're forever secure.

P.S. An interesting fact about bamboo:
Bamboo has a higher tensile strength than many alloys of steel, making it incredibly strong and durable despite its lightweight appearance. This unique property has led to the use of bamboo in various construction projects, including the creation of sustainable and sturdy buildings, bridges, and even ladders in many parts of the world. It's a testament to nature's engineering brilliance and the versatility of this incredible plant.

Bamboo, with its slender, resilient stems that gracefully reach for the sky, stands as a symbol of nature's strength and adaptability. Its rapid growth and unwavering flexibility remind us to bend without breaking, offering valuable life lessons through its quiet and enduring presence.

Dreamscape

In the silence of my sleep, where time stands still,
The world seems so vivid and yet so real.
Dreams dance like whispers in the midnight air.
Leaving traces of memories beyond compare.

Sometimes, in the depths of weary minds,
A dream takes hold, and the effect binds
Long after I woke, it still held my way.
A cherished fragment; in my mind, it'll stay.

Crystal clear, like a painting in my mind,
I weave the tale for all who lend an ear.
With eager hearts, I share its vibrant hue.
A glimpse of magic—that, to me, is true.

Oh, how I long to decode its code.
To understand what lies beneath its hold,
For dreams, they speak in an unknown tone.
Not revealing the secrets that are mine alone

Yet, in the pursuit of meaning and truth,
I may lose sight of the dream's sacred youth,
For dreams are free, unbound by rational thought,
It whispers softly in the silence I've sought.

Let me revel in their enchanting spell.
Embrace the mystery it weaves so well,
In these dreams, I find a moment's grace.
A glimpse of heaven in this earthly space

And as the dream remains sculpted in my soul,
A very precious gift, forever I'll remember,
Dreams are the windows to my heart.
Guiding me when life tears me apart.

I'll cherish every dream that graces my sleep.
Hold me close, for in my heart I'll keep
And let its beauty light my waking hours,
Dreams, you are my life's most treasured flowers.

P.S. While exploring dreams' mysterious allure, I invite you to delve deeper into the scientific realm of dreams. Have you ever wondered about the science behind dreams? Knowable Magazine offers an enlightening article on the subject, unraveling the intricate tapestry of our subconscious minds. Feel free to share your thoughts, experiences, or insights about dreams and the intriguing aspects they hold. Have dreams ever sparked your curiosity or prompted you to seek a deeper understanding?

Quote: "Dreamscape: Where the Blossom Holds the Key to My Life's Most Precious Memories."

Scripted by Fate

Life is really unpredictable sometimes.
We plan to get the best outcome.
Yet our hearts remain dissatisfied.
Yearning for something more, something
profound.

But lo and behold, an unexpected wind blows,
From the depths of the unknown, it softly flows.
Bringing with it the most beautiful outcome,
Where our hearts find solace, a place to call
home.

In that moment, we realize what truly matters:
All the waiting, the longing, the scattered

For in this unexpected breeze, we find,
A sense of satisfaction and a peaceful mind.

Life's twists and turns, its ebbs and flows,
They lead us to places we never chose.
But by surrendering, we find our way.
Leaving to God the role we must play.

For He, the Almighty, knows what's best,
His hand guided us through each test.
So let go, dear heart, and trust in His plan.
For the unexpected wind is where true joy can
stand.

Embrace the unpredictability of this existence,
Seek the winds of change with persistence.
And when you find that moment to truly live,
Acknowledge it as God's artwork and offer
thanks.

P.S. Have you ever found a moment of true fulfillment or unexpected joy in a situation that didn't go according to your plans? How did that experience impact your perspective on life's unpredictability?

Quote: “Amidst life’s unpredictable winds, the most beautiful destinations are often reached through unplanned journeys.”

Which Holds My Heart: The Right or the Left?

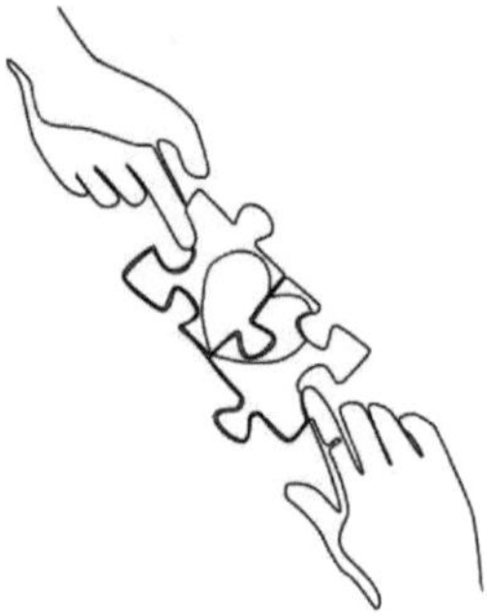

In a moment of innocent curiosity,
A child asks their mother, with tender plea,
"Amma, whom do you love the most, me or my brother?"
And the mother, wise and gentle, ponders another.

Before answering, she poses a query:
"Which eyes do you love, my dear?
The right or the left, can you really say?"
The child, perplexed, couldn't find a way.

"How can I choose between my faithful eyes?
When are both a part of me, a heavenly prize?
I love them both, without a doubt.
For together they bring the world about."

With a gentle smile, the mother then reveals,
"My answer, my baby, is as your heart feels.
Just as you cannot separate your sight,
I love you both with all my might.

To you and your brother, my precious two,
Are pieces of my soul, forever true.
You both came from me, a love so pure.
In my heart, you'll forever endure."

And so the child understands,
That love knows no boundaries or demands.
In the embrace of a mother's affection,
Both siblings find solace and protection.

For in this world, where love can mend,
We find unity, a bond that transcends.
The love of a mother, unwavering and strong,
A melody that carries us along.

So let us cherish, with hearts ablaze,
The love that guides us through life's maze.
For in the embrace of a mother's grace,
We find our truest selves in this sacred space.

P.S. Have you ever experienced a similar tender moment with your parents or guardian? Share an instance where you asked a heartfelt question and received a cherished response filled with love and wisdom.

Quote: Love knows no bounds; it embraces each part equally, just as a mother cherishes each child.

A Walk in the Dark

In the stillness of dawn, before the world awakens,
I step out into the darkness, my pug by my side.
At 5 o'clock, the perfect hour for our daily stroll,
No traffic hinders, just a cool breeze to guide.

We wander down the familiar road we tread so often.
Each step falls softly, echoing the rhythm of our hearts.
The darkness envelops us like a comforting shield.
No fear, no hesitation—just a sense of peace imparts.

This morning feels different; the darkness seems deeper.
It's as if a thick veil has descended over our path.
No street lamps, no stars in the sky, and darkness everywhere,
Only a single light shines brightly in front of my gate.

In the absence of any glimmer of light, we dare to walk.
As our path is known, we walk day and night.
So we walk with no fear, cutting through the darkness.
Walking with ease, like drifting through a dream with closed eyes.

After walking so long in darkness, we plan to go back,
But as I turn back, I see the light from my gate.
A small beam of hope, dispelling the weight,
In the darkness, a glimmer of possibility shines.

It dawned on me then, in that moment of clarity,
Life may be a journey through shadows and strife,
But a simple turn backward can reveal the way.
A ray of hope, a flicker of light, guides us through life.

I walk on with renewed faith and determination.
Embracing the darkness but never losing sight,
Even in the toughest of moments, there's always a hope.
To illuminate our path and lead us towards the light.

So walk on, dear friend, with hope in your heart.
Even in the darkness, there's a fresh start.
Just turn around, and you will see,
The light that shines is eternally free.

P.S. As you journey through life's darkest moments, remember that even a single flicker of hope can illuminate your path and guide you towards brighter days ahead. Keep faith, and never lose sight of the light that shines within you.

Question for the Readers: What does the image of the single light shining in the darkness symbolize for you? How does it resonate with your own experiences or beliefs?

Quote: "Even when walking towards darkness, just remember, a simple turn around can reveal the light."

What, Why, and How??

In this house, where curiosity painted the walls,
I found happiness in the answers to my unending
"what," "why," and "how" questions.
Inspired by my dear children.

We shared an eternal dance to the music of
inquiry.
Their relentless curiosity tests my patience at
times.

Yet filling this home with vibrancy. As they
entered their teenage years,
A subtle transformation took place.
Daily enquiries vanished.

Leaving me with only those precious moments
of curiosity that once satisfied me.
The silence became a canvas longing to be
filled.
With the brushstrokes of their curious voices.

Realizing how deeply I missed those questions,
Which once felt endless,
I chose to reverse the roles.

I embraced the art of curiosity.
Posing my own "what," "why," and "how"
questions to my children,
With eagerness in my heart.

I knew this was the way to preserve those
treasured moments.
To keep our connection thriving.

My children, appreciating the significance of
these questions,
Responded with thoughtful and heartfelt
answers.

In this exchange, we nurtured a connection,
That transcended mere inquiry.
Creating a beautiful connection of
understanding.

It left me content and surrounded.
By the answers to my "what," "why," and "how."

In this house, where curiosity dwelled,
We found happiness in the dance of questioning
A dance that brought us closer,
And filled our lives with wonder and fulfillment.

P.S. Curiosity became my secret ingredient for staying connected with my kids. What's your special recipe for family bonding? Share your tales of connection and curiosity with us!!

Spine in the Desert

In a plain vast and green,
Where life's wonders are seen,
A love story begins to fly.
In the sky, where dreams lie.

Once bushy and green, the cactus stood,
In the plain, she wandered into the wood,
She fell for the sun's golden shine.
In a land where love is fine.

But the sun, bright and bold,
Couldn't shine in every fold.
So cactus, with love so true,
Asked, "Where do you shine bright and true?"

"The desert," replied the sun,
"Where my rays burn as one."
Without a pause, cactus pledged,
"On your side, I'll be edged."

Yet the sun warned of the heat.
The desert's scorching beat,
But cactus, with all her might,
Chose to bask in love's light.

"I'll shed my leaves," she said.
"To stand by you with all my stead."
And so, with spines in place,
Their unconditional love continued an eternal grace.

P.S. This tale, born of my imagination, now rests in your hands for consideration. As you delve into its imaginary world, I'm curious: what emotions did it evoke? Which scenes ignited your imagination? Your insights are invaluable, guiding the evolution of my storytelling craft.

Quote: True love is like a cactus in the desert, embracing the sun's scorching heat and still blooming with unwavering devotion.

A Facade Tore Me Deep

In the midst of a bustling, noisy street,
Outside the grocery store, I stood in the heat.
A whirlwind of emotions swept over me,
A woman approached to tell her story with a
plea.

Wrapped in a torn saree, tears on her cheeks,
Her plea for help pierced through the noisy
streets.
"My child's unwell," she sobbed in despair.
Her voice trembling, her heart in pain

Without pause, I reached into my pocket deep,
A 200 rupee note, a token to reap.
To ease her burden, if just for a while,
A moment of warmth to her sobbing heart.

But as she hurried off, a nudge in my chest,
A 500 rupee note, a thought with just,
To offer her more, a help with care
But fate intervened with a twist in the air.

Deceived by the illusion of a mother in need,
I saw the woman, and my heart began to bleed.
In front of a cigarette shop, her true intentions revealed.
The trust I had extended, now shattered and peeled.

Disillusionment left wounds tearful,
A painful lesson, a bitter realization,
How to trust again to those in need?
Kindness met with betrayal, a bitter seed.

Yet within the depths of my guarded heart,
A flicker of compassion refuses to depart.
For though darkness may shadow and trust may wane,
Kindness still echoes through joy and pain.

This is not alone my story, many fooled too,
But still, kindness wins, hearts anew.
Hearing sobbing tales, hands still extend,
Sometimes greeted with joy, sometimes betrayal's blend.

PS: Think about how the themes of trust and kindness in the poem relate to our everyday interactions. Why do we still choose to help others even when we know there's a risk of being let down? Have you ever faced a situation where your trust was challenged, and how did it affect your willingness to lend a helping hand?

Quote: "Sometimes we get caught in the whirlwind of how people act, forgetting to see who they truly are beneath the facade."

Why is it so easy for us?

Since I can remember, from the very beginning,
She only lived for others.
Nothing for her, just thinking of us all the time.

Though she's faced countless situations,
She knows how to give us luxury out of that
She has all the solutions always ready in hand

For every stressful question,
Just turn to her.
Even she takes our burden as well.

She never claims anything for herself.
All she wishes for is our happiness.
Still, she is wishing the same.

The most talented creative lady turned to nothing.
Just because she kept us in everything,
The world cannot value her treasure.
As she never displays it to anyone.

She set aside her passion, her creativity,
And every inch she loves,
Just to take care of us and love us.
Many times, we simply overlook her.
But the reality is that we should praise her for everything.
As they are very rare in the world,
Who are willing to drop their dreams just for our sake.

We never value her tears, her sadness, or her joy.
As she always ignores them for us,
These us never value her.

Why is it so easy for us to forget her teachings?
Why is it so easy for us to ignore all her feelings?

If we are sad, then it's sad.
But when she is sad,
There is no other way; she needs to take care of us.

Why such big discrimination towards her?
Why does this 'us' stop her from flying?

It's the fault of "us" who made her this way.
This "she" is nothing but my mom,

To whom I never valued,
She is nothing but my God.

P.S. Let these words serve as a gentle reminder: How will you honor the silent strength of the one who always puts you first?

Quote: "Why is it so easy for us to ignore you?" "Why is it so easy for you to love us unconditionally?" A question from her kids to a mother.

A Dance Caught My Mind!

Early in the morning, I woke up before the sun.
The very first thing, open the window and let the cool breeze run.
With a cup of coffee in hand, each sip savored slow,
Time slipped away without me even knowing how.

The sun peeked through, signaling the start of the day,
But I wanted just a moment more to let my coffee stay.
I was about to complain, "Why are you so early, my dear sun?"
But then I saw the quantum dust, a dance had begun.

Nature choreographed a mesmerizing display,
Quantum dust and sunbeams in a sink they did play.
I was struck by the beauty, the energy, and grace,
Words spilled from my mouth, in awe of their embrace.

I reached for my phone to capture this sight,
But the brilliance escaped me, in the sun's blinding light.
No worries though, the memory in my mind engraved,
A scene of pure beauty, in which I was saved.

What a joy to witness, the dance of dust and sun,
In a sink they twirled, their performance begun.
I disrupted their rhythm, but they quickly fell back in line,
A beauty so profound, it's hard to define.

This moment of magic, a gift from the dawn,
A reminder to start the day with energy and brawn.
Though words may fall short, in capturing the scene,
The dance of quantum dust, forever in my dreams.

PS: As I enjoy the morning's beauty, reflecting on the dance of quantum dust and the warmth of morning coffee, I'm reminded of the fleeting beauty that surrounds us each day. Let us cherish these small moments of wonder and find joy in the simple pleasures that life offers. May the memory of this enchanting dance linger in our minds, inspiring us to embrace each new day with gratitude and a sense of awe.

Have you ever experienced a moment of unexpected beauty or wonder that left a lasting impression on you? What was it like, and how did it make you feel? Share your thoughts and reflections with us.

Quote: "Look at the golden sun rays, peeking through the window, gently caressing my face, as if to whisper, 'Wake up, my dear, for another day waits for you'."

I Am Trapped!

Trapped in my thoughts, I feel so alone.
In a cage of darkness, all on my own.
No ray of hope, no joy or pain,
It's just never-ending, suffocating rain.

Lost in a sea of sadness and despair,
My emotions and feelings are beyond repair.
The darkness consumes me as a whole,
Leaving empty, a hollow soul.

My smile, my tears, and my happiness are gone.
All taken by these thoughts, one by one.
I cry out for help, but no one hears.
Lost in this darkness, consumed by fears.

They've taken everything from me,
First my smile, then my glee.
No tears left to cry,
As I watch time fly,
I'm drowning in this dark sea.

I wander aimlessly in this void.
No sense of time, no feelings enjoyed.
Drowning in darkness, suffocating within,
Please, someone save me; help me begin.
In silence, I scream, trapped in my mind.
I am praying for a ray of light to find.
Emptiness looms, and darkness persists.
Burning me in the darkest fuel, my thoughts
resist

I beg for release, for a way out.
From this never-ending cycle of doubt.
Please help me escape, set me free,
This cage of thoughts is consuming me.

In this endless night, I search for dawn.
Hoping against hope, I'll soon be drawn.
Out of this darkness, into the light,
Breaking free from this eternal plight.

But until that day, I'll continue to roam.
Trapped in my thoughts, longing for home.

A prisoner of my own mind, lost without
knowing the way,
I'm waiting for someone to show me the way.

PS: In the depths of our own struggles, it's all too easy to miss the silent cries for help from those around us. They may not articulate their pain in words, but it resonates in the shadows of their eyes and the weight of their sighs. Day by day, inch by inch, they find themselves ensnared in the labyrinth of their thoughts, yearning for a flicker of light to guide them out of the darkness.

But do we see it? Are we tuned in to the silent pleas echoing in the depths of their souls? Let's pause, listen, and extend a hand of empathy to those silently grappling with their demons. In our willingness to truly see and understand, we may become the beacon of hope they desperately seek.

When will you finish?

Lost in a state of mindless bliss,
Floating at the top of cold water,
Weightless and free, like a feather.
But then a sound disrupts the peace,
"When will you finish?" A question comes,
And I am pulled back to reality,
Drowning in the icy depths,
A heavy burden is pressing me down.

Why is it always me,
To be yanked from serenity,
Plunged into chaos and stress?
The question haunts me,
Echoing in my every thought,
A constant reminder of my shortcomings,
A never-ending cycle of doubt.

I long to stay in that state of weightlessness,
To never have to face the harshness of the world,
But I am always reminded,
That I cannot escape forever,
That I must face the challenges,
And find a way to rise above,
To break free from the chains that bind me.

So I push myself through the freezing waters,
Struggling against the current,
Fighting to find my way back to the surface,
To find that fleeting moment of peace,
Before once again being pulled under,
With the never-ending question,
"When will you finish?"

In life's ever-changing game,
The question may shift, but it's all the same.
In whispers soft or voices bold,
Its weight endures, and its grip takes hold.
So amidst the chaos, stay true,
For the struggle persists, whatever you do.
Remember this, when the day is through,
In different forms, it calls, but the battle continues.

P.S. Take a moment for yourself amidst life's busy waves. Remember to be gentle with your own heart. How will you make room for self-care in your daily hustle?

Quote: "Amidst the chaos, try to take time for you, for the struggle persists, whatever you do."

A Word So Deep: Sonder

Understanding "Sonder":
"Sonder" refers to the profound realization that everyone around us has a life as rich and complex as our own. It's a word that captures the interconnectedness of humanity and the importance of empathy and understanding. Through the lens of "sonder," we gain a deeper appreciation for the shared experiences and struggles that bind us together.

It's a story of my childhood days,
I was a student struggling in many ways.
After school, for tuition, I would go.
A routine that I came to cherish and know.

Each day, a routine of rushing to and fro,
But amidst the chaos, a moment of pure joy,
Walking towards tuition, learning and grow,
Then back again, with friends to enjoy.

Always early for class, always late coming home
These moments of enjoyment, a treasure to me
Time rushed by like a whirlwind,
But in these moments, I found peace.

A woman by her gate, staring my way,
Day after day, without a word to say,
I felt her eyes, piercing and cold,
A mystery that I could not unfold.

Months passed, and still, she'd stand and stare,
I felt her gaze, a weight I couldn't bear,
Hating her stare but never asking why,
Judging her in silence, letting assumptions fly.

Sickness struck me, a week away from my path,
Her concern was raised, scared and confused
She came to the tuition center, seeking me out,
To my home, she just came, without a doubt.

As she shared her story, her tears in the bath,
I saw her in a new light, with open eyes.
Ready to listen, that awaited tale,
Her tears spoke volumes, her face so pale.

She had a daughter once, carefree like me,
But sickness stole her away, leaving her alone,
My presence, a balm, a sight to see,

A medicine to calm her, to set her free.

In that moment of truth, I learned something new,
Not to judge a book, by its cover, so wrong. The philosophy of sonder, a lesson so grand,
To acknowledge the inner worlds, hand in hand.

In the streets of my childhood, I learned lessons so grand,
Taught by a woman, with a gentle hand,
To embrace the unknown with an open heart,
In the whole stages of life, to play our part.

P.S. Delve into the depths of "sonder" as you go through the lines of this poem. How has your perception of human connection been shaped by the realization that each harbors a world as complex as your own?

Quote: "Everyone you meet has a story that is slightly different but just as complex as your own, filled with its own twists and turns."

My Crafted Steps

In thinking of the future, a plan took shape
To build a staircase of dreams, a path to take
Research by hand, ingredients gathered tight
Bricks of hard work and discipline in the light

Laying a foundation, a line so straight
Cemented with confidence, a step to create
As the sun rose high, the day turned to night
Rest needed—a pause in the fight

But while I slept, in a world of dreams,
Someone came by and watered my schemes.
The next day, a surprise awaited with might,
My steps were strong, basking in the light

With more determination now, I continued to build
Each step is a journey, and each moment fulfilled
Days turned to years, and the staircase grew tall
Closer to success, with each step I'd install

Yet in my focus on the path well-known
I forgot about those who helped but have never shown.
To water my steps, to make them secure.
To climb with firmness, to keep me sure.

In the journey of crafting, we often forget
To thank those who helped us set
Our steps to success in a world so vast
Grateful to those who helped us last

So let's remember, as we climb each day
The ones who watered, the ones who paved the way
The staircase to success is not a solo flight
But it's a collective effort to reach the light.

PS: As you reflect on the journey depicted in "My Crafted Steps," consider this: Who are the people in your life who have watered your dreams and helped you along your path to success? Take a moment to appreciate their contributions and share your thoughts in the comments below.

Quote: "A well-crafted stair to success is the culmination of hard work, determination, and the collective support of all who knowingly and unknowingly helped pave the way."

Oh My God, Take A Break!

In the early morning light, my daughter's question
Echoes in the quiet of our home:
"Amma, does God listen to everybody's prayers?"
Without hesitation, I assure her,
"Yes, sweetheart, he hears every plea."

But then, her innocent insight:
"She just asked God to get tired each day, right?"
I pause, pondering her words.
"Yes," she continues, "during assembly time,
The whole school prays, even Principal Mam.
Oh my God, your life is more miserable than ours."

Her empathy pours forth,
Acknowledging the weight of His burden,
Listening to the cries of all,
And offering solace to each weary soul.
"You're always busy," she worried.
"I fear you won't even rest or eat or sleep."

A pang of guilt pricks my heart
As I listened to her tender plea:
"Okay, God, today at least, take a break,
And let no prayers disturb Your peace.
But in this world of urgent needs,
Please listen to my plea, selfish though it may seem,
To postpone my test, my greatest need."

And then, a promise, sincere and true:
"I won't trouble You tomorrow, I swear."
In her small voice, a world of compassion:
"I'll pray that everyone else postpones their prayers too,
So you can have a well-deserved break."

In her words, a melody of childlike grace,
A glimpse of faith in its purest place,
A selfless wish in a sacred space,
A reminder of innocence, a divine embrace,
Her tender plea, a lesson to embrace.

P.S: "Inspired by a conversation with my daughter, this poem explores the innocence, empathy, and faith of a child's perspective on prayer and the divine. May it remind us all of the beauty in simple acts of compassion and the importance of nurturing faith in our hearts."

Question to readers: "What are your thoughts on the role of empathy and compassion in our relationship with the divine? How does this poem resonate with your own experiences or beliefs about prayer and faith?"

Quote: "Childhood innocence: where prayers are simple and hearts are pure. And they say, 'God, take a break, I know you're tired'."

Just Us!

In the calm of the afternoon,
after a satisfying meal,
I head to my favorite spot.
There, I eagerly wait for my special friend.

He comes quietly, like a soft whisper.
His touch brings warmth and comfort, easing my mind.
With him, time slows down.
and worries disappear.

Even on days when I'm loaded with work,
Our love for each other overcomes all problems.
It's just us, lost in peace and happiness.

I welcome his embrace.
feeling light and serene.

Together, we enter a dreamy world.
leaving reality behind.

It's during these moments, amidst the chaos, that our bond strengthens,
and our connection deepens.

I value him dearly.
In his company,
I find joy and renewal.

Every day, I look forward to our time together.
knowing he'll bring me comfort and happiness.

And who is this beloved friend?
It's none other than my dear nap,
my trusted companion in moments of rest and calm.
Many share this deep affection
for this humble yet invaluable delight.

P.S. Just us, dear reader, in the realm of tranquility and repose, where the world fades into the background and only the gentle rhythm of our breath remains. May you always find solace and rejuvenation in the simple joys of life, whether it's through a cherished nap or any other peaceful moment that brings you comfort.

What moments of tranquility do you cherish in your own life, and how do they bring you peace amidst the chaos of everyday living?

Quote: "Love to be in those precious moments, when all fades away, only the steady rhythm of the heart remains: lub-dub, lub-dub." Oh! What a peace…

Emotional Elegance

Women's Day Tribute
In life's big story, women stand tall,
Feeling all emotions, whether big or small.
Their smiles light up even the darkest night,
Spreading joy and hope—oh, what a sight!

With tears in their eyes, they tell stories true,
Of sadness and strength, seen by me and you.
When anger flares up, they demand respect,
A power in their eyes, no one can reject.

Love, sweet love, in their touch we find,
Healing hearts broken, being ever so kind.
But carrying a weight, deep down they bear,
Emotions they handle with such tender care.

Handling emotions gently, day by day,
Women guide feelings in their own special way.
Women, like weavers, in life's grand design,
Expressing emotions, pure and fine.

PS: On this Women's Day, let us honor the emotional elegance of women everywhere, who weave the fabric of life with grace and resilience. May we celebrate their strength, their wisdom, and their unwavering ability to express the depths of their souls with effortless majesty. Today and every day, let us stand in awe of the incredible contributions of women as they continue to inspire and uplift us all. Happy Women's Day!

Ignored The Presence

In the serenity of a beautiful garden,
A butterfly danced with elegance.
Its delicate wings fluttering with grace.

Nearby, a flower swayed gently in the breeze.
Its colorful petals basking in sunlight.
Highlighting its vibrant beauty.

Each time they crossed paths,
The butterfly and flower pretended not to notice each other.
An unspoken distance unknowingly lingered between them.

Rooted to the ground, the flower displayed its beauty.
While the butterfly flitted from bloom to bloom,
Existing in separate worlds within the same space.

As the days turned into weeks, time passed by.
The flower and butterfly are busy on their own paths,
Lost in a solitary existence, unknowingly.

But in separation, their bond grew stronger.
Whispering the same sentiment into the breeze,
From opposite ends, 'I can't live without you'.

PS: As you reflect on the intertwining dance of the butterfly and the flower, consider: What invisible threads connect us to those we seemingly ignore, and what hidden emotions lie beneath the surface of our interactions?

Quote: "Once, when I stood beside you, you never met my gaze. Now, miles apart, you whisper, 'I want to be with you.' The irony of distance reveals the true essence of longing."

A Wild Journey of Parenthood

Ah! Parenthood's first steps, a wild ride,
In a dense jungle, with nothing but a bag by our side.
As parents, we stumbled through and through.
Yet within that bag, we had the solutions to grow.
Caring for our child in the best way we know.

Time passed; another child in our hands we
hold.
The bag's contents were used again, and stories
were retold.
For the second, like Mowgli, we played the part.
In the wild, unafraid, with courage in our hearts.
Living freely, wild, and bold.

In the adventurous wild life we thrive,
Enjoy each moment and feel alive.
Reflecting on the past, we can't deny
How scared we were to enter this jungle, Oh
my!
Now, pros, knowing every nook and cranny, we
fly.

This is parenthood with one or two.
Where we roam freely with no limits and no
clues.
In the vast wilderness of raising children,
Navigating through challenges, hearts unshaken,
With love as our compass, memories guide our
view.

Oh, the wild journey of parenthood!
We now enjoy staying in the woods.
In the heart of the jungle's embrace,
Together in its untamed grace.
As parents, wild and free, we just run the race.

P.S. In the end, amidst the wilderness of parenthood, remember to cherish every moment, for the journey is as precious as the destination. May your jungle journey be filled with love, laughter, and endless adventures.

What is your favorite metaphor for describing the experience of parenthood, and why does it resonate with you?

A Kindness and its Miracle

In a small town, a girl grew into a woman
Uncertain of her path, faces rejection at every turn.
Praying for a miracle to guide her way,
Wishing for a ray of light to brighten her day.

But one day, the heavens heard her plea,
A job offer arrived, setting her free.
Gratitude swelled deep within her soul.
For this unforeseen blessing, she could now hold.

Years passed, and the truth was revealed.
Of a young girl's kindness, profoundly sealed.
In her school days, she noticed a boy in need.
And without hesitation, she offered to feed.

Sharing her lunch daily, a gesture beyond compare,
An act of kindness destined to spread and share.
Little did she know the impact she made.
Would come back to her in such a beautiful shade.

The boy she helped, now a successful man,
Remembered her kindness with a helping hand.
Offered her a job, a chance to shine,
Without unveiling their bond, a gesture so fine.

Acts of kindness, no matter how small,
It can change lives; break down every wall.
Lunches shared those days, a miracle grown.
Compassion's power is forever shown.

This is the tale of a girl and a boy.
Of kindness and fate, of hope and joy.
What may appear small can truly expand.
A giver's kindness is a miracle for the receiver's hand.

PS: As you reflect on the intertwining paths of kindness and miracles within this tale, consider: What small act of kindness have you performed or experienced that you believe could spark a miraculous chain of events?

Quote: "An act of kindness from one end is not just a gesture; it's a miracle for the one in need, illuminating paths and warming hearts along the way."

A Venomous Creeper

Deep inside me lies a calm garden.
Where dreams and hopes sparkle under the sun.
Yet lurking there, a Venomous Creeper,
With its tendrils of anger, jealousy, negativity, and despair.

Every day, I feel its grip tighten.
Trying to crush my dreams relentlessly.
Though I shield them with care and love, it's hard.
For the Venomous Creeper's strength is formidable.

But I won't surrender.
I seize its dark vines, refusing defeat.
Instead of letting it destroy my dreams,
I harness its energy to grow stronger.

With each step I take,
The Venomous Creeper's grip weakens.
Instead of hindering, it propels me forward.
Fueling new ideas and creativity.

Now, my garden blooms,
Each dream stands tall, filled with hope.
As I nurture with inspiration,
Peace and happiness fill my soul.

From my darkest depths,
I've cultivated a garden of creativity.
Though the journey was challenging,
My determination made transformation possible.

The Venomous Creeper's seeds turned into inspiration,
Through challenges, I persevered.
With steadfast resolve,
I've emerged stronger than before.

PS: Remember, within the darkest shadows lie the seeds of our greatest strength. Embrace the challenges, for they are the fertile ground from which our dreams bloom.
What strategies do you employ to overcome negative emotions and obstacles in pursuit of your dreams?

Quote: "Embrace the transformative power of venom; sometimes, it serves as the antidote to save lives. Extracting positivity from negativity shields us from its harmful effects, ensuring it cannot reflect upon us."

Click, click!!

On Valentine's Day, when love fills the air,
A couple ventures out, a night to share,
They ordered special food—a cake so sweet,
To make this occasion truly complete.

But as they wait, their phones they hold,
Scrolling through screens, lost in that space,
Unaware of time passing by so fast,
Neglecting the moments meant to last.

The food arrives, and the cake follows with it.
Click, click!! Eagerly capturing images,
Post them online for the world to see.
Their eyes remain fixed on the phone's screen.

Within seconds, messages flooded their screens.
Wishing them love, as if in their dreams.
They read and replied, absorbed in the glow.
Unaware of food getting cold slow and slow.

Thus, their celebration, carefully planned,
Lost in the scroll, a moment slipped.
In just a fraction of carelessness, they lost,
Missing special moments, at such a cost.

Oh, this tale of you and me, my dear,
Caught in the merry-go-round of scrolling.
Let us pause, let us cherish, let us embrace.
The beauty lies in spending time together.

PS: Inspired by countless reels online showcasing the beauty of love and the pitfalls of digital distraction. Let's use this reminder to cherish the present moment and prioritize genuine connection over the virtual world. As you reflect on this poem and its message, ask yourself: In what ways can I prioritize genuine connection and presence in my relationships amidst the distractions of the digital age?

Quote: "Fully cherish life's most precious moments, lest they slip away with the click of a distraction."

Oh! You, The Attention Seeker

In the deep of night, as sleep holds me tight,
You come, uninvited, a silent breeze so light.
You gently touch me, hoping I'll notice, I might,
But I'm lost in my dreams; your pleas lost tonight.

Yet you persist, a whisper against my ear,
I recognize you, oh I do, but pretend not to hear.
Still I turn away, craving peaceful sleep.
A quiet mind, a soft bed, your whispers to cease.

You relent, for a moment, leaving me be,
But oh, you attention seeker, you're not yet free.
You need my focus, my acknowledgment to thrive,
If I refuse, you sneak into my dreams and strive.

From the depths of sleep, you take hold, a grip so tight,

Your presence can be felt, like a shadow in the night.
Each passing minute, you tighten your grasp,
In a silent battle, a breath, a gasp.

But that's not enough, is it? You demand to be felt,
To consume my thoughts, in my mind to melt.
Oh, you attention seeker, your needs grow more,
Until tears stream down my face, more wet than before.

A silent acceptance of your presence, your pain,
Your touch, your grip, your emotional rain.
Yet, even as I surrender, you release your hold,
With that, I embrace sleep, your story untold.

You slip away, leaving just the echo of your touch,
You depart without a word; my peace matters that much.
Yet, I know you'll return, waiting for another chance,
Waiting patiently, ready to advance.

Oh, you persistent attention seeker, Migraine!
You make your claim again and again.
In the deep of night, you seek the spotlight's gleam,

But for now, let me rest, let me dream.

PS: For those who battle migraines, you may find solace in knowing you're not alone in this struggle. Keep fighting for moments of peace and relief amidst the storm.

Have you ever experienced a situation where a physical ailment felt like an attention-seeking presence in your life? How did you cope with it?

Quote: "In the quiet battle against pain, determination to endure whispers louder than suffering."

Not A Magic But A Science Behind!

In warm kitchens, where pots and pans reside,
A mother cooks with her children by her side.
Cartoons hum in the background, voices blend,
Their laughter fills the air—a joyful trend.

Though unseen, the screen, she hears the words,
Tales of heroes, friendships, and tears stirred.
Each episode, character, and scene,
Etched in her mind, like a vivid dream.

"We've seen this one before!" she'd say,
Her children marvel at her memory's sway.
But it's not just recall; it's more than that.
The power of the mind, a mental act.

So the children paused with curious ask,
"How do you know of these shows, this task?"
"I listen while I work," she said with a cheer.
Their wonderment drawing her near.

And so, when asked how, she knows it all.
She whispers with a smile, "The power of recall."
But little ones, it's not just memory's grace.
It's the magic of mental imagery in its place.

For in our minds, we hold the key,
To painted pictures and stories so free.
These mental visions linger long,
In the chambers of our hearts, where memory belongs.

Let us cherish this gift, this power within,
Turning words into images, making them kin.
For it's not magic, but science at play,
A testament to the wonders of our brain's display.

As you read, imagine the scene so bright,
Mother and kids—a heartwarming sight.
It's the power of the mind in every way,
Your thoughts echo the same—a smile for the day.

PS: Mental imagery not only aids in memory formation but also enriches our understanding and perception of the world. By engaging our imagination, it allows us to create detailed mental representations of scenes, events, and information, often surpassing the vividness of direct sensory experiences. This phenomenon highlights the incredible power and versatility of the human mind in processing and retaining information.

Quote: "Sometimes, the most powerful images are not those we see with our eyes, but those we create with our minds through the magic of words and sound."

Framed With Our Own Minds!

Framed with our own minds, a tale we never knew
Desires leading us down paths to insecurities anew.
"Buy three, get one free," luring us with its call,
Promises we believe, only to realize we fall.

Banners of savings, a tempting piece to seize,
We yield to the offer, caught in the breeze.
In hindsight, truth unfolds, our desires exposed,
Manipulated, controlled, our wills imposed.

We need one, yet we take all three,
Choosing what's not essential, all for free.
But nothing truly comes without a fee,
Each "free" item, a cost we fail to see.

Cautionary tale we all have heard,
Our desires can lead us, leave us blurred.
In realization, a lesson is found,
Be mindful; make choices sound.

Yet in this realization, a lesson we unearth,

Be mindful, aware, of our own self-worth.
Empowered to make choices that are crystal clear,
Navigating temptations without a hint of fear.

An age-old story, retold once more,
We are the architects of our own fate, that's for sure.
Avoid the unseen trap before it's too late,
Walk with clear eyes; shape your own fate.

P.S. Life's daily hustle can draw us in with tempting offers and quick rewards. But it's important to stop and think about the true cost of our choices amidst the chaos. Those flashy promotions often conceal hidden costs – draining our finances, emotions, or sense of self.

By staying mindful of our desires and values, we empower ourselves to make decisions that truly reflect who we are. Let's learn from the past and carry that wisdom forward as we journey into the future, with clarity and determination guiding our way.

Quote: ‘Buy two, get two free'—a trap where we fall, paying for all four when only one was our true need.

Why My Love?

In the vast expanse of my heart, my love poured out.
Yet, alas, it never echoed back, casting doubt.
With courage, I approached love's radiant light.
But the world's weight pulled me back into the night.

My love, boundless and free, knows no boundaries,
Yet weighed on scales with all worldly worries.
Not reasoned, but from the core of my heart it flows.
Yet unfairly judged, it's true depth nobody knows.

Why, oh why, must my love face such
harshness?
Endlessly giving, receiving naught but darkness.
Lost within love's maze, shadows cloak my way,
Through ceaseless nights and days, my love is
on display.

But why does my love linger unseen, unheard,
unfelt?
Why, oh why, does it seem lost, like a treasure
never dealt?
In shadows of love's maze, bewildered, I roam,
As my love yearns for a place to find its home.

P.S. This poem reflects the heartfelt journey of unrequited love, questioning the fairness of its treatment and seeking understanding in the midst of uncertainty and longing.

Quote: "In a world where love is the sole language spoken, there my love was left unheard, unseen, and unfelt. Sadly, it now appears lost in the passage of time."

My Naughtiness and Her Smile

In a classroom filled with laughter and jest,
There dwelled a naughty kid, always putting his teachers to the test.
His jokes flowed like a river, never-ending and sly,
Earning him a reputation that reached for the sky.

One day, his teacher, with frustration in her eyes,
Asked him a question that took him by surprise.
"How does your mother handle you?" she demanded to know,
As his mischievous grin continued to glow.

With a twinkle in his eye, he replied without delay,
"My mom, you see, is a beauty in every single way.

They say her beauty shines through when she smiles,
And she smiles the most when I'm cracking my jokes."

"Behind every successful naughtiness of a kid," he went on with a grin,
"There's a mother's smile, supporting from within."
The teacher, unable to contain her laughter, had to admit,
"Sometimes, perhaps, there may be some truth in it."

So let us remember, in every mischievous child's game,
There's a mother's smile, silently cheering his name.
For in that smile lies a love so pure and true,
Guiding and praying for their safety in all that they do.

P.S. This poem was born from a simple conversation with my child about his mischievous adventures in the classroom. His casual response lingered in my mind, its sincerity resonating deeply within me. When I asked him why he gave such an answer, he simply replied, "I meant it." And as a smile spread across my face, he confirmed, "Yes, I was right." Such genuine moments remind us of the profound truth behind the simplest of words and actions. They encapsulate the pure love and authenticity that flow between parent and child, shaping our understanding of life's meaningful connections.

Reflecting on your own childhood, what memories do you associate with your mother's smile in response to your mischievous behavior?

Quote: In every playful child's game, there is a mother's smile, silently praying for their safety and cheering their names.

A Story Without Words

Every day, I pass you by, your face concealed,
Behind a mask, your identity is sealed.
Yet, your eyes, captivating and bright,
They weave tales, painting pictures in the light.

No words are spoken, but a bond we share,
Through silent gazes, a connection rare.
Amidst bustling crowds, I seek your gaze,
Eager to decipher today's mystic tale.

Your eyes, a bundle of emotions to decode,
Sometimes warm, sometimes cold.
Sometimes elicit smiles, sometimes draw out sighs,
A window to secrets, where emotions fly.

In eager anticipation, I await,
To decode the tales your eyes create.
In the hustle and bustle, I search for a sign,
Yearning to claim the next chapter, to make it
mine.

The curiosity your eyes ignite,
Draws me closer, in the busy street with light.
Though strangers we are, your eyes, my friend,
With every look, a journey together we ascend.

I dream of the day our eyes will meet,
And from that glance, my heart will beat.
To see myself reflected in your eyes one day,
That's my dream—to be a story without words,
in every way.

P.S. This poem is a product of my imagination, exploring feelings and relationships through fictional writing. Even though the characters and events are not real, they're inspired by how people connect in real life. I hope readers can still understand and relate to the themes of understanding and empathy in the poem, even though it's not based on actual experiences. It serves as a reminder of how important it is to understand each other, even without words, in our daily lives.

As you read this poem, think about times when you've felt a strong connection without uttering a single word. Consider your own experiences with silent moments and how they've affected the way you see relationships.

Quote: "Some of the most beautiful stories are those that remain unspoken yet resonate deep within our hearts."

Thank You

To my dear readers,

Thank you for embarking on this poetic journey with me. Your support and encouragement mean the world to me. Each poem in "Treasured Echoes" is a piece of my heart, and I am grateful for the opportunity to share these moments of reflection and introspection with you.

May these verses inspire you to pause, reflect, and find beauty in the quiet moments of your life. Your presence in this journey enriches my creative path and fills it with purpose.

With heartfelt gratitude,

Divya Shiji

9 789363 318403

Printed by Libri Plureos GmbH in Hamburg, Germany